Dear Sam.

Some houses are built without walls

A little light
reading for you...

Much love,

Carla
xxx

11/05/22

***

This book
is dedicated to all the silenced souls
within the archives

***

Some houses are built without walls

Sara Levy

Clayhanger Press
2021

We're all in the dumps,
For diamonds are trumps ;
The kittens are gone to St. Paul's !
The babies are bit,
The moon's in a fit,
And the houses are built without walls.

Typeset in Garamond

First Printing, 2021

Published by Clayhanger Press
7 Highfield Court
Newcastle under Lyme
Staffordshire
ST5 3LT
www.clayhangerpress.co.uk

ISBN-13: 978-1-7398007-4-1

Clayhanger Press

Acknowledgements

I would like to thank Rebecca Jackson and her colleagues at the Staffordshire Record Office for facilitating my access to the Staffordshire Asylum record archives, Lucy Smith of Keele University for her assistance and advice regarding the archive, the contributors to the blog site 'A Case for the Ordinary'; and the staff of the Staffordshire Archive and Heritage Service for allowing me access to their asylum artefacts.

The images on pages 22 (ref. 7369/1) and 25 together with the background images in the erasure poems are reproduced with the kind permission of Staffordshire Record Office.

I am grateful to Newcastle University for funding my research trip to Stafford, and for the sage advice and warm encouragement of my tutors Tamar Yoseloff and Glyn Maxwell.

Thanks too to my patient editor Roger Bloor, my mentor and sounding board Vanessa Lampert and my fellow MA students who workshopped some of these poems in their early stages.

My copies of The Slang dictionary (Chatto & Windus, 1891) and The Nursery Rhyme Book (F. Warne & Co., 1897) were invaluable reading whilst these poems were developing, and they have enriched my writing.

Thank you finally to Lauren, Paul and Seb; your love, support and belief in me is what keeps me going.

Contents

Sew the Button on

To jot down at once what you wish to remember, lest it be lost or forgotten
(Brewer's Phrase & Fable, 1894)

frayed at the edges   thoughts   u n r a v e l l i n g
coming   apart   at   the   seams   lose the thread
embroider the truth patch the holes
hanging on by a thread
unpick   the   truth
button your lip
I am undone
hemmed in
stitched up
cross my
h e a r t
h o p e
to die
stick
a
n
e
e
d
l
e
i
n
m
y
e
y
e

Extract from the
Rules of the Commissioners in Lunacy.

(Issued 26th June, 1895, to come into operation on 1st September, 1895.)

10.—The entries in the medical journal, case books, and *post mortem* book, to be kept in every institution for lunatics shall be made by the medical officer thereof, or by an assistant medical officer under his supervision and control, and every such entry shall be signed or initialed by the person making the same.

11.—The prescribed entries in the medical journal to be kept in institutions for lunatics shall be made once in every week, or, in the case of a licensed house at which visits by a medical practitioner at more distant intervals than once a week are permitted, at each visit.

12.—Within seven days after the admission of a patient there shall be entered in the medical case book for patients the following particulars :—

(a) A statement of the name, age, sex, and previous occupation of the patient, and whether married, single, or widowed, and a copy of the statement of facts contained in the medical certificates accompanying the reception order.

(b) An accurate description of the external appearance of the patient upon admission :—of the habit of body, and temperament; appearance of eyes, expression of countenance, and any peculiarity in form of head; physical state of the vascular and respiratory organs, and of the abdominal viscera, and of their respective functions; state of the pulse, tongue, skin, etc.; and the presence or absence, on admission, of bruises or other injuries.

(c) A description of the phenomena of the mental disorder :—the manner and period of the attack, with a minute account of the symptoms, and the changes produced in the patient's temper or disposition; specifying whether the malady displays itself by any, and what delusions, or irrational conduct, or morbid or dangerous habits or propensities; whether it has occasioned any failure of memory or understanding; or is connected with epilepsy, or ordinary paralysis, or general paralysis.

(d) Every particular which can be obtained respecting the previous history of the patient :—what are believed to have been the predisposing and exciting causes of the attack; what were the previous habits, whether active or sedentary, temperate or otherwise; whether the patient has experienced any former attacks, and, if so, at what periods; whether any relatives have been subject to insanity or other nervous disease or phthisis; whether the present attack was preceded by any and what premonitory symptoms; and whether the patient has undergone any, and what, previous treatment, or has been subject to restraint of personal liberty.

13.—Subsequent entries describing the course and progress of the case, and recording the medical and other treatment, with the results, shall be made in the case book for patients at the times hereinafter mentioned, that is to say: once at least in every week during the first month after reception, and oftener when necessary; afterwards in recent or curable cases, once at least in every month, and in chronic cases, subject to little variation, once in every three months. But all special circumstances affecting the patient, including seclusion and mechanical restraint, and all accidents and injuries, must be at once recorded. A printed copy of this and the last preceding rule shall be inserted at the beginning of every case book for patients.

What place is this?

O THAT I was where I would be,

    then would I be where I am not !

   But where I am, why, there I must be,

      and where I would be, I cannot.

What place is this?

    I pace the room, speak

   with various items of furniture

      concerning my inheritance

a fortune will come to me

    once I have the will

   I must climb up this chimney

    for a copy is hidden here.

What place is this?

    a house built without walls?

   I was mistaken. There is

    no furniture

 no chimney

Reasons for admission

Because 16 children
Because painful hair
Because voices in the walls
Because found her husband hanged
Because vagina is a devil to be fed
Because a dog surprised him
Because lost at heaven's gates
Because ruined hopelessly
Because gunpowder beneath the bed
Because poison in the porridge
Because death of a child
Because angels come to whip him
Every night
Every night

Refectory, Cheddleton asylum

We sit on benches after the mutton
and cabbage are cleared away,
the smell of it hanging heavy
and we watch as the attendants
count each piece back in,
locked up in a wooden box
and handed out as if it was gold:
knives, forks, spoons all
accounted for, so fearful
of the harm we might do.
There are women in here
with tongues sharper
than these refectory knives
and the forks are as blunt
as a baby's first comb.
Every mealtime an old woman
hides a knife inside her dress
and is made to hand it back,
and there's a story told
of a fellow who swallowed
a spoon once and died.
Now we're obliged to sit here
and wait for the reckoning.

Lost Notes

The Music Professor would sit at the asylum piano, play the most complex
of Handel concertos, filling the corridors with such sweet melodies
wrung from the keys at phenomenal speed, as the Holy Spirit
and angels chattered, the voices of all the dear departed
prattled on like a restless, fidgeting concert audience
hot fingers sweeping the piano keys to deaden
the drone of cacophonous noises until
doctors agreed that a blood-letting
might be employed to calm his
composure, steady the mania
slow down his music from
tumbling torrents rapids
the raging of rivers
babbling brooks
to a stream of
semi quavers
trickles of
crotchets
bubbled
one by
one
he
saw
them
pool
in
the
little
dish
his
dark
tadpoles
minims of sound
                  each
         note
                        bled
away
               into

                          silence

Visiting Day

The shame of it.
Briskly off loaded
from the train
at a place they call
Lunatics Junction
to a tramcar that edges
steep up the incline
dragging us gaggle
of visitors, nervously
clutching our gifts
home-made pies,
knitted socks, sketches
of little box houses
four windows, smoke
chimney, from children
who ask *when will daddy
come home?* No one
makes small talk.
Fingers twist shawls,
we eye with suspicion
our carriage companions
do they have it too,
in their blood?
As the tram clears
the crest of the hill
that first glimpse –
bigger, much bigger
than ever imagined.
Grand like a palace
of madness, a giant brick
wasps' nest, humming
with chaos. Asylum.
Even the word
makes me shudder.

Letter 1.

What vile stuff

Mag. Sulph. Mist. Sennae Co. Lig. Amon. Acet. fort. Tr.
Cinchonae Co. Chlorodyne (1885) Lin. Camph Co. Syr.
Hypophos. Co. Pot. Iod. Pulv. Am. Carb. Sod. Salicyl. Glyc.
Bellad. Inf. Senega. Conc. Inf. Gent. Conc. Tr. Nucis. Vonc. Ac.
Sulph. dil. Phenacetin tablets. Pil. Blaud. Hospital Strapping
(Leicester) Medicine bottles 6 oz. Mist. Expectorans. Conc.
Bismuth Carb. Castor Oil. Seidlitz Powders. Tr. Digitalis. Lin.
Terebinth. Mag. Carb. L. Spt. Methyl. Lig. Morph. Hydro. Cyllin.

what vile stuff   injected my husband
make so ghastly   mr grainger   no morphia
kept   but worse drugs exist   if happens
not convinced   natural death   no doubt   committee
think   silenced me   ignoring   letters   refusing but
fight not knocked out   yet laughing at me
you trump cards   my   case home secretary
winning to the end   god   another life beyond
all reckoned   await reply   what injected why

Aromat. Pulv. Ac. Boric. Boric Lint. Carbolized Tow. Cyanide
gauze. 2oz. bottles. Fumigating Pastilles. Tr. Capsicum. Lig.
Plumbi. Subacet. fort. Zinci Ox. Pulv. Ac. Boric. Liq. Ferri.
Perchlor. Fort. Ac. Carbolic. pur. Ferri. et Am. Cit. Ext. Cascara.
Liq. Trional 20grs powders. Pil. Col. Co. Mag. Sulph. Iodoform.
Bellad. plaster. Mag. Cit. Eff. Lig. Bismuth et. Am. Cit. Lin. Iodi.
Quin. Hydrochloride. Spt. Chlorof. Spt. Etheris. Pot.
Brom. Quin. Am. Aq. Calcis. Vin. Ipecac. Spt. Methyl. Syr.

The Examination Room

Upon admission, patient was found to be in frail health,
and unresponsive to basic questions

      Doctor enters the room, his maggot words
drop to the floor, ignored.
I am listening to him with my teeth.
      I hover like a bluebottle
above this almost corpse
         as doctor searches for the distant
crackle of breath in the foamy bellows
prods the pale tripe of slack belly
pulls back the shuttered lids
      peers in
             a vacant room
table scrubbed almost white
          chipped bowl
a piece of spoiled meat
              a fly

Letter 2.

Burn this

I hope that you have mended your gloves and jacket. By the way, is the size of the gloves 6 ½? I must know your answer. Don't wear red in either hats or bonnets, it is too common. Being true to oneself is so very important, having fully made up one's mind. What delightful weather we are having. It is only fit for snow-balling. Don't you agree with me that it is a long time to wait? Burn this letter. I was separated from my wife a full two years before I was made a lunatic. Hoping you are not vexed or annoyed by this lengthy communication. I think it is important to be off with the old love before one is in with the new. Do you not agree? The last time I stopped to talk to you for just two minutes I remarked that the other fellows would miss me but what am I supposed to do? Decision is everything in these dark days. It is quite possible that I may leave this place soon. Burn this letter. I have only been in six such places, and I have stayed longer than I usually stop. I came here on someone's birthday. Unless I receive a plain yes or no I must consider the matter closed, for time flies. Are you quite decided? Except on the grounds of any assumed lunacy am I not entitled to an answer? It is of the greatest importance to me, at least, I think so, judging by the complicated state of my mind. In Spring, a young man's fancy turns to things of love. I have a slight cold. Could you send me Coleridge's poems? The doctor knows what I intend to do and has agreed that I may consult with a solicitor. Love is a sacred feeling. This is my stern reality. I await your answer. Burn this letter please

My eye

quiet at my embroidery
I promise you I am at my most dangerous,
Muther, I am thinking –
when I hold the metal up to the light,
the better to thread the yarn
peer through the eye of that needle
and fix you in my gaze
through the small aperture
I am looking directly into your soul
through the small aperture
and fix you in my gaze
peer through the eye of that needle
the better to thread the yarn
when I hold the metal up to the light,
Muther, I am thinking –
I promise you I am at my most dangerous,
quiet at my embroidery

Extract from the
Rules of the Commissioners in Lunacy.

(Issued 26th June, 1895, to come into operation on 1st September, 1895.)

10.—The entries in the medical journal, case books, and *post mortem* book, to be kept in every institution for lunatics shall be made by the medical officer thereof, or by an assistant medical officer under his supervision and control, and every such entry shall be signed or initialed by the person making the same.

11.—The prescribed entries in the medical journal to be kept in institutions for lunatics shall be made once in every week, or, in the case of a licensed house at which visits by a medical practitioner at more distant intervals than once a week are permitted, at each visit.

12.—Within seven days after the admission of a patient there shall be entered in the medical case book for patients the following particulars :—

(*a*) A statement of the name, age, sex, and previous occupation of the patient, and whether married, single, or widowed, and a copy of the statement of facts contained in the medical certificates accompanying the reception order.

(*b*) An accurate description of the external appearance of the patient upon admission :—of the habit of body, and temperament ; appearance of eyes, expression of countenance, and any peculiarity in form of head ; physical state of the vascular and respiratory organs, and of the abdominal viscera, and of their respective functions ; state of the pulse, tongue, skin, etc. ; and the presence or absence, on admission, of bruises or other injuries.

(*c*) A description of the phenomena of the mental disorder :—the manner and period of the attack, with a minute account of the symptoms, and the changes produced in the patient's temper or disposition ; specifying whether the malady displays itself by any, and what delusions, or irrational conduct, or morbid or dangerous habits or propensities ; whether it has occasioned any failure of memory or understanding ; or is connected with epilepsy, or ordinary paralysis, or general paralysis.

(*d*) Every particular which can be obtained respecting the previous history of the patient :—what are believed to have been the predisposing and exciting causes of the attack ; what were the previous habits, whether active or sedentary, temperate or otherwise ; whether the patient has experienced any former attacks, and, if so, at what periods ; whether any relatives have been subject to insanity or other nervous disease or phthisis ; whether the present attack was preceded by any and what premonitory symptoms ; and whether the patient has undergone any, and what, previous treatment, or has been subject to restraint of personal liberty.

13.—Subsequent entries describing the course and progress of the case, and recording the medical and other treatment, with the results, shall be made in the case book for patients at the times hereinafter mentioned, that is to say : once at least in every week during the first month after reception, and oftener when necessary ; afterwards in recent or curable cases, once at least in every month, and in chronic cases, subject to little variation, once in every three months. But all special circumstances affecting the patient, including seclusion and mechanical restraint, and all accidents and injuries, must be at once recorded. A printed copy of this and the last preceding rule shall be inserted at the beginning of every case book for patients.

stone mother

there is a   in everything
oh yes   it is here
they say   a child
but   nothing
but i have felt   for days
i cannot remember   i got here
the doctors say i   a child
they tell me i must   a while
rest until i am   again
if i am confined   these walls
this place is   now
let it heal the   in me
let it be my   stone mother

Andrew Grant, aged 20, proselytizer

God spoke to me

From New York to England, I pilgrimed the ocean
pushed on by faith and fair weather.
I preached as I travelled, bible in hand,
Spreading the word of God as it came to me,
clear as a bell in the night.

Fulfilling my mission, I spoke outside taverns,
in town squares, on market days, waylaying passers-by,
stopping the shoppers and sharing the scriptures,
charged with the task of saving each soul
in the towns that I toured.

Children threw stones at me, innkeepers
cursed me for scaring off trade, I was pilloried,
laughed at, my language grew stronger, my sermons
more desperate, why were they turning
their backs on salvation?

My liturgies deemed a disturbance.
Arrested, I passed from prison to workhouse
but would not stop praying and seeking forgiveness
for those that derided me, would not be parted
from my one prized possession,

would not put it down when I reached the asylum,
fearing God might forsake me, not for doctors
or nurses, not when they sat me in front of a camera,
and the devil said *come fella, hands in your lap now
there's a good chap. let go of the Bible. Be still.*

I Am

I am cutting holes in water

Am I already dead?

I am Beelzebub's daughter

Am I tomorrow to be wed?

I am drowning here forever

Am I a lunan lost?

I am searching for my treasure

Am I the Holy Ghost?

I am wisps of smoke on water

Am I dressed in clothes on fire?

I am a lamb to slaughter

Am I dancing on the spire?

I am here but know not where this is

I am here but I am lost.

lunan, archaic word for young girl

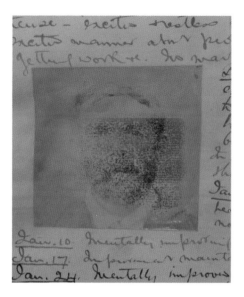

Walking in the grounds I met a man

with bees buzzing in his head
could hear the hive swarming
and I listened as he asked his queen
what should he say to me
amber swirling behind his eyes
those eyes of liquid honey
and his smooth skin tattooed
every inch with small hexagons
warm honey churning behind his eyes
head humming with bees
and his queen whispering to him
whispering to walk away.

☞ Largest and Finest Bio-Cinematograph and Dissolving Views in the United Kingdom.

Mr. R. P. GOODACRE, F.R.S.G.S.

Will give an

EVENING'S ENTERTAINMENT

Consisting of

Rome, Naples and Pompeii

Being a Tour through Italy.

The Second Part of the Entertainment consists of

ANIMATED PICTURES

BY THE

Bio-Cinematograph

Popular Subjects.

The Latest Invention of the 19th Century. Size of Views 15 feet 6 inches by 10 feet 6 inches. Illustrated by the Newly Invented Ejector Jets, 600 Candle Power.

SEASON 1903-04.

Staffordshire County Council.

Cheddleton Asylum,

LEEK.

TUESDAY, December 8th, 1903.

Commencing at   o'clock.

BRITTAN WAKELIN, PRINTER, ALFORD.

Dissolving views in the evening, a tour of the animated asylum, commencing at   o' clock.

Empty cloud faces stare in the airing court
Pacing out circles, all foggy eyed
dream walkers dragging their heels.

But at night, minds like birdcages open
and dormitories hum with excitement
a chatter of chaffinches, flutter of memories

fretting lost children, the setting on fire
of petticoats, spit in the eye of a woman who
looks at you askance –

the whispering blasphemies, eyes in the walls
that are watching you, plans being hatched
to poison the porridge, despatch you.

Take off your clothes for the devil is sewn
in the lining, your pockets are burning,
your head's full of feathers and fishermen

hidden beneath beds quite invisible waiting
with nets to pounce and surprise you
hook out your eyes

you smuggled a bottle of Chloroform,
cut holes in the water, lost hold of your daughter,
purchased a ticket to heaven and sought her.

Grief, aged 23

Alice Maud May on a chair in a room
she is no longer part of,
stares as the angels brush past her head.
They are holding a baby,
can pass the child angel to angel mid-air
with effortless grace.
Alice looks on as her baby is cradled,
silver thin ribbons make
figures of eight and glide into ether.
Stars light up the walls.
Ears full of music that no one but she
can hear, Alice waits,
willing the angels to reach down, raise her
up from this room.

Joseph Challinor steps out

through his skylight, grabs fistfuls of night, fingers

reach for the pin-headed stars, scales the rooftop deft

as an acrobat, finding her window unlatched.

Come dawn Ellen kisses the love-addled lad from her bed,

dismisses him to sky walk his way home. She knows these trysts

risk too much. Soon this madness must end.

She sends back his love letters, bolts shut her window.

Red-eyed and raging he curses her, curses each man that dares

look at her, retreats to the rooftop to sit in despair

swings his legs from the parapet, tells the deaf stars

of his heartbreak, her callousness, drops stone after stone into darkness

and smiles as they smash to the courtyard below

stares at the lunatic moon, looming bigger tonight, so close

he could stand up and stroll off to join it so one last time

Joseph
        steps out

                         into air.

Dead indeed

This news was the talk of the airing courts.
The soft lad that fell for nurse Bentley,
Left a letter and sovereigns for his three
Orphaned children may God rest his soul.

For a ha'penny token, Elizabeth May
Will show you the place where his body lay
Mangled. She likes the word.
Rolls it around like a marble.
Mangled she laughs,
Points to the roof and then to the path -
Fell seventy feet like a stone from above.
An asylum's the place to go mad with love.
And when your heart begins to bleed,
You're dead, and dead, and dead, indeed.

Letter 3.

Blood line

gentlemen about thirty years ago the late john xxxx died in the county asylum quite mad so i am told and his brother there also will you please inform me if it is carried in the blood as i am married to his son and have every reason to think my husband is going the same way i am at my wits end and have had cause to report his behaviour to the police who bid me to enquire as to whether there in insanity in the family you must understand me sirs there is to be a child

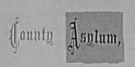 
19th MARCH, 1901.

Programme of Vocal & Dramatic Recital

BY

MR. & MRS. WALLIS A. WALLIS,

Of the Crystal *Palace, Queen's Hall, London, New York, Chicago, etc.*

FIRST MOVEMENT ...	"Tragic" Symphony ...	...	*Schubert*
DUET	... "Langsyne" ...	...	*A. A. Needham*
SONGS	{ "Only" { "A Corn Song" }	...	...*Coleridge Taylor*

MR. WALLIS.

RECITATION ...	"A Ballad of East and West" ...	...	*Kipling*

MR. WALLIS.

SONGS	"Good Bye" ...	... ...	*Schlesinger*
	"Sing Throstle Sing"	... ...	*A. Borton*
HUMOROUS STORY ...	... ...	...	..

MR. WALLIS.

SELECTION	"Yeoman of the Guard"	... ...	*Sullivan*
FIVE SHORT SONGS ...	... ...	... ...	*F. Lambert*

1. *"Tis Night."*
2. *"Love in* Absence.*"*
3. *"A Barque at Midnight."*
4. *"The night has* a thousand eyes.*"*
5. *"One more clasp."*

MR. WALLIS.

MUSIC POEM ...	"The Story of a Faithful Soul" ...	...	*A. Proctor*

Music by Stanley Hawley. MRS. WALLIS.

DUETS	"Is it the Wind?" ...	*Villiers Stanford*
	"Barcarolle"	...*Chaminade*
SECOND MOVEMENT	"Tragic" Symphony	*Schubert*
RECITAL	Dramatic Scenes from the Comedy (in Costume.)	

"THE HUNCHBACK,"

By SHERIDAN KNOWLES. Scene 1, Act 4. Part of Scene 1, Act 5.

CHARACTERS } Helen ... ... MRS. WALLIS.
 Modus... ... ... MR. WALLIS.

LAST MOVEMENT ...	"Tragic" Symphony ...	...	*Schubert*

The seamstress's lament

Had you but paid
A thimble full of heed
To what I said

I might not be here
My love, and you
Might not be dead

Author's notes

This pamphlet began as a poetry research project within the archives of the Staffordshire Record Office, focussing on the 19th century admission books, correspondence and photographs from three Staffordshire mental asylums. While the use of terms like 'mental asylum', 'lunatic' and 'madness' are incompatible with our modern day understanding of mental ill health, the language of the poems is copied directly from the archives and reflects an earlier, less enlightened time.

The poems *Joseph Challinor* and *God Spoke to Me* feature real people and real events, other poems draw from reports and ledgers, and quote the words of doctors and patients. In *Reasons for admission,* only lines found within the pages of the admissions books have been used.

Themes of missing or confused memories recur throughout the archive, and have been represented in many of the poems in the form of gaps, spaces and fracture lines, which also attempt to denote the silencing of patient's voices, and their invisibility once they had been incarcerated. This use of erasure resurfaces in the redaction poems. Taking an existing text from the archive; rules, posters and entertainment programmes, and layering new colour to reduce the transparency of the original text, a poem is created by rubbing away in places to reveal words. This peeling away of layers mimics the researcher's task, which is to work in a vast archive, only scratching the surface.

Extracts from contemporary nursery rhymes are woven throughout the book, and these are denoted in italics.

Typesetting & Design Roger Bloor

Proof-Reading Adam Lampert

www.clayhangerpress.co.uk

Printed in Great Britain
by Amazon